Meal Planner

NOTES

Family Favorites

Family Favorites

Breakfast and Lunch

Snacks

Breakfast Ideas

Lunch Ideas

Notes

Meal Plan

DATE:

MONDAY

NOTES

TUESDAY

NOTES

WEDNESDAY

NOTES

THURSDAY

NOTES

FRIDAY

NOTES

WEEKEND

NOTES

Breakfast Ideas

Lunch Ideas

Notes

Meal Plan

DATE:

MONDAY

NOTES

TUESDAY

NOTES

WEDNESDAY

NOTES

THURSDAY

NOTES

FRIDAY

NOTES

WEEKEND

NOTES

Breakfast Ideas

Lunch Ideas

Notes

Meal Plan

DATE:

MONDAY

NOTES

TUESDAY

NOTES

WEDNESDAY

NOTES

THURSDAY

NOTES

FRIDAY

NOTES

WEEKEND

NOTES

Breakfast Ideas

Lunch Ideas

Notes

Meal Plan

DATE:

MONDAY

NOTES

TUESDAY

NOTES

WEDNESDAY

NOTES

THURSDAY

NOTES

FRIDAY

NOTES

WEEKEND

NOTES

Breakfast Ideas

Lunch Ideas

Notes

Meal Plan

DATE:

MONDAY

NOTES

TUESDAY

NOTES

WEDNESDAY

NOTES

THURSDAY

NOTES

FRIDAY

NOTES

WEEKEND

NOTES

Breakfast Ideas

Lunch Ideas

Notes

Meal Plan

DATE:

MONDAY

NOTES

TUESDAY

NOTES

WEDNESDAY

NOTES

THURSDAY

NOTES

FRIDAY

NOTES

WEEKEND

NOTES

Breakfast Ideas

Lunch Ideas

Notes

Meal Plan

DATE:

MONDAY

NOTES

TUESDAY

NOTES

WEDNESDAY

NOTES

THURSDAY

NOTES

FRIDAY

NOTES

WEEKEND

NOTES

Breakfast Ideas

Lunch Ideas

Notes

Meal Plan

DATE:

MONDAY

NOTES

TUESDAY

NOTES

WEDNESDAY

NOTES

THURSDAY

NOTES

FRIDAY

NOTES

WEEKEND

NOTES

Breakfast Ideas

Lunch Ideas

Notes

Meal Plan

DATE:

MONDAY

NOTES

TUESDAY

NOTES

WEDNESDAY

NOTES

THURSDAY

NOTES

FRIDAY

NOTES

WEEKEND

NOTES

Breakfast Ideas

Lunch Ideas

Notes

Meal Plan

DATE:

MONDAY

NOTES

TUESDAY

NOTES

WEDNESDAY

NOTES

THURSDAY

NOTES

FRIDAY

NOTES

WEEKEND

NOTES

Breakfast Ideas

Lunch Ideas

Notes

Meal Plan

DATE:

MONDAY

NOTES

TUESDAY

NOTES

WEDNESDAY

NOTES

THURSDAY

NOTES

FRIDAY

NOTES

WEEKEND

NOTES

Breakfast Ideas

Lunch Ideas

Notes

Meal Plan

DATE:

MONDAY

NOTES

TUESDAY

NOTES

WEDNESDAY

NOTES

THURSDAY

NOTES

FRIDAY

NOTES

WEEKEND

NOTES

Breakfast Ideas

Lunch Ideas

Notes

Meal Plan

DATE:

MONDAY

NOTES

TUESDAY

NOTES

WEDNESDAY

NOTES

THURSDAY

NOTES

FRIDAY

NOTES

WEEKEND

NOTES

Breakfast Ideas

Lunch Ideas

Notes

Meal Plan

DATE:

MONDAY

NOTES

TUESDAY

NOTES

WEDNESDAY

NOTES

THURSDAY

NOTES

FRIDAY

NOTES

WEEKEND

NOTES

Breakfast Ideas

Lunch Ideas

Notes

Meal Plan

DATE:

MONDAY

NOTES

TUESDAY

NOTES

WEDNESDAY

NOTES

THURSDAY

NOTES

FRIDAY

NOTES

WEEKEND

NOTES

Breakfast Ideas

Lunch Ideas

Notes

Meal Plan

DATE:

MONDAY

NOTES

TUESDAY

NOTES

WEDNESDAY

NOTES

THURSDAY

NOTES

FRIDAY

NOTES

WEEKEND

NOTES

Breakfast Ideas

Lunch Ideas

Notes

Meal Plan

DATE:

MONDAY

NOTES

TUESDAY

NOTES

WEDNESDAY

NOTES

THURSDAY

NOTES

FRIDAY

NOTES

WEEKEND

NOTES

Breakfast Ideas

Lunch Ideas

Notes

Meal Plan

DATE:

MONDAY

NOTES

TUESDAY

NOTES

WEDNESDAY

NOTES

THURSDAY

NOTES

FRIDAY

NOTES

WEEKEND

NOTES

Breakfast Ideas

Lunch Ideas

Notes

Meal Plan

DATE:

MONDAY

NOTES

TUESDAY

NOTES

WEDNESDAY

NOTES

THURSDAY

NOTES

FRIDAY

NOTES

WEEKEND

NOTES

Breakfast Ideas

Lunch Ideas

Notes

Meal Plan

DATE:

MONDAY

NOTES

TUESDAY

NOTES

WEDNESDAY

NOTES

THURSDAY

NOTES

FRIDAY

NOTES

WEEKEND

NOTES

Breakfast Ideas

Lunch Ideas

Notes

Meal Plan

DATE:

MONDAY

NOTES

TUESDAY

NOTES

WEDNESDAY

NOTES

THURSDAY

NOTES

FRIDAY

NOTES

WEEKEND

NOTES

Breakfast Ideas

Lunch Ideas

Notes

Meal Plan

DATE:

MONDAY

NOTES

TUESDAY

NOTES

WEDNESDAY

NOTES

THURSDAY

NOTES

FRIDAY

NOTES

WEEKEND

NOTES

Breakfast Ideas

Lunch Ideas

Notes

Meal Plan

DATE:

MONDAY

NOTES

TUESDAY

NOTES

WEDNESDAY

NOTES

THURSDAY

NOTES

FRIDAY

NOTES

WEEKEND

NOTES

Breakfast Ideas

Lunch Ideas

Notes

Meal Plan

DATE:

MONDAY

NOTES

TUESDAY

NOTES

WEDNESDAY

NOTES

THURSDAY

NOTES

FRIDAY

NOTES

WEEKEND

NOTES

Breakfast Ideas

Lunch Ideas

Notes

Meal Plan

DATE:

MONDAY

NOTES

TUESDAY

NOTES

WEDNESDAY

NOTES

THURSDAY

NOTES

FRIDAY

NOTES

WEEKEND

NOTES

Breakfast Ideas

Lunch Ideas

Notes

Meal Plan

DATE:

MONDAY

NOTES

TUESDAY

NOTES

WEDNESDAY

NOTES

THURSDAY

NOTES

FRIDAY

NOTES

WEEKEND

NOTES

Breakfast Ideas

Lunch Ideas

Notes

Meal Plan

DATE:

MONDAY

NOTES

TUESDAY

NOTES

WEDNESDAY

NOTES

THURSDAY

NOTES

FRIDAY

NOTES

WEEKEND

NOTES

Breakfast Ideas

Lunch Ideas

Notes

Meal Plan

DATE:

MONDAY

NOTES

TUESDAY

NOTES

WEDNESDAY

NOTES

THURSDAY

NOTES

FRIDAY

NOTES

WEEKEND

NOTES

Breakfast Ideas

Lunch Ideas

Notes

Meal Plan

DATE:

MONDAY

NOTES

TUESDAY

NOTES

WEDNESDAY

NOTES

THURSDAY

NOTES

FRIDAY

NOTES

WEEKEND

NOTES

Breakfast Ideas

Lunch Ideas

Notes

Meal Plan

DATE:

MONDAY

NOTES

TUESDAY

NOTES

WEDNESDAY

NOTES

THURSDAY

NOTES

FRIDAY

NOTES

WEEKEND

NOTES

Breakfast Ideas

Lunch Ideas

Notes

Meal Plan

DATE:

MONDAY

NOTES

TUESDAY

NOTES

WEDNESDAY

NOTES

THURSDAY

NOTES

FRIDAY

NOTES

WEEKEND

NOTES

Breakfast Ideas

Lunch Ideas

Notes

Meal Plan

DATE:

MONDAY

NOTES

TUESDAY

NOTES

WEDNESDAY

NOTES

THURSDAY

NOTES

FRIDAY

NOTES

WEEKEND

NOTES

Breakfast Ideas

Lunch Ideas

Notes

Meal Plan

DATE:

MONDAY

NOTES

TUESDAY

NOTES

WEDNESDAY

NOTES

THURSDAY

NOTES

FRIDAY

NOTES

WEEKEND

NOTES

Breakfast Ideas

Lunch Ideas

Notes

Meal Plan

DATE:

MONDAY

NOTES

TUESDAY

NOTES

WEDNESDAY

NOTES

THURSDAY

NOTES

FRIDAY

NOTES

WEEKEND

NOTES

Breakfast Ideas

Lunch Ideas

Notes

Meal Plan

DATE:

MONDAY

NOTES

TUESDAY

NOTES

WEDNESDAY

NOTES

THURSDAY

NOTES

FRIDAY

NOTES

WEEKEND

NOTES

Breakfast Ideas

Lunch Ideas

Notes

Meal Plan

MONDAY

NOTES

TUESDAY

NOTES

WEDNESDAY

NOTES

THURSDAY

NOTES

FRIDAY

NOTES

WEEKEND

NOTES

Breakfast Ideas

Lunch Ideas

Notes

Meal Plan

DATE:

MONDAY

NOTES

TUESDAY

NOTES

WEDNESDAY

NOTES

THURSDAY

NOTES

FRIDAY

NOTES

WEEKEND

NOTES

Breakfast Ideas

Lunch Ideas

Notes

Meal Plan

DATE:

MONDAY

NOTES

TUESDAY

NOTES

WEDNESDAY

NOTES

THURSDAY

NOTES

FRIDAY

NOTES

WEEKEND

NOTES

Breakfast Ideas

Lunch Ideas

Notes

Meal Plan

DATE:

MONDAY

NOTES

TUESDAY

NOTES

WEDNESDAY

NOTES

THURSDAY

NOTES

FRIDAY

NOTES

WEEKEND

NOTES

Breakfast Ideas

Lunch Ideas

Notes

Meal Plan

DATE:

MONDAY

NOTES

TUESDAY

NOTES

WEDNESDAY

NOTES

THURSDAY

NOTES

FRIDAY

NOTES

WEEKEND

NOTES

Breakfast Ideas

Lunch Ideas

Notes

Meal Plan

DATE:

MONDAY

NOTES

TUESDAY

NOTES

WEDNESDAY

NOTES

THURSDAY

NOTES

FRIDAY

NOTES

WEEKEND

NOTES

Breakfast Ideas

Lunch Ideas

Notes

Meal Plan

DATE:

MONDAY

NOTES

TUESDAY

NOTES

WEDNESDAY

NOTES

THURSDAY

NOTES

FRIDAY

NOTES

WEEKEND

NOTES

Breakfast Ideas

Lunch Ideas

Notes

Meal Plan

DATE:

MONDAY

NOTES

TUESDAY

NOTES

WEDNESDAY

NOTES

THURSDAY

NOTES

FRIDAY

NOTES

WEEKEND

NOTES

Breakfast Ideas

Lunch Ideas

Notes

Meal Plan

DATE:

MONDAY

NOTES

TUESDAY

NOTES

WEDNESDAY

NOTES

THURSDAY

NOTES

FRIDAY

NOTES

WEEKEND

NOTES

Breakfast Ideas

Lunch Ideas

Notes

Meal Plan

DATE:

MONDAY

NOTES

TUESDAY

NOTES

WEDNESDAY

NOTES

THURSDAY

NOTES

FRIDAY

NOTES

WEEKEND

NOTES

Breakfast Ideas

Lunch Ideas

Notes

Meal Plan

DATE:

MONDAY

NOTES

TUESDAY

NOTES

WEDNESDAY

NOTES

THURSDAY

NOTES

FRIDAY

NOTES

WEEKEND

NOTES

Breakfast Ideas

Lunch Ideas

Notes

Meal Plan

DATE:

MONDAY

NOTES

TUESDAY

NOTES

WEDNESDAY

NOTES

THURSDAY

NOTES

FRIDAY

NOTES

WEEKEND

NOTES

Breakfast Ideas

Lunch Ideas

Notes

Meal Plan

DATE:

MONDAY

NOTES

TUESDAY

NOTES

WEDNESDAY

NOTES

THURSDAY

NOTES

FRIDAY

NOTES

WEEKEND

NOTES

Breakfast Ideas

Lunch Ideas

Notes

Meal Plan

DATE:

MONDAY

NOTES

TUESDAY

NOTES

WEDNESDAY

NOTES

THURSDAY

NOTES

FRIDAY

NOTES

WEEKEND

NOTES

Breakfast Ideas

Lunch Ideas

Notes

Meal Plan

DATE:

MONDAY

NOTES

TUESDAY

NOTES

WEDNESDAY

NOTES

THURSDAY

NOTES

FRIDAY

NOTES

WEEKEND

NOTES

Breakfast Ideas

Lunch Ideas

Notes

Meal Plan

DATE:

MONDAY

NOTES

TUESDAY

NOTES

WEDNESDAY

NOTES

THURSDAY

NOTES

FRIDAY

NOTES

WEEKEND

NOTES

Breakfast Ideas

Lunch Ideas

Notes

Meal Plan

DATE:

MONDAY

NOTES

TUESDAY

NOTES

WEDNESDAY

NOTES

THURSDAY

NOTES

FRIDAY

NOTES

WEEKEND

NOTES

Made in the USA
Middletown, DE
09 October 2023

40470757R00064